# Teach Your Dog
# CORNISH

At last, my dog and I will be able to understand each other, and perhaps some light will finally be shed on the whole fox poo debacle...
I realise I shouldn't have rolled in it.'

*DAWN FRENCH*

Pyth yw hanow da rag ki yowynk?

*KOLYN (PUPPY)*

Anne Cakebread not only has the best name in the Universe, she has also come up with a brilliantly fun book which will help humans and canines learn new languages.

*RICHARD HERRING*

# Teach Your Dog

# CORNISH

Anne Cakebread

Thank you to:
Helen, Marcie, Frieda and Lily, my family,
friends and neighbours in St Dogmaels
for all their support and encouragement,
Carolyn at Y Lolfa, and Dr Talat Chaudhri
and Tony Hak for Cornish translations
and pronunciations.
Meur ras dhywgh.

*First impression 2019*

© Anne Cakebread & Y Lolfa Cyf., 2019

Illustrations and design by Anne Cakebread

ISBN: 978-1-912631-10-0

Published and printed in Wales on paper from well-maintained
forests by Y Lolfa Cyf., Talybont, Ceredigion SY24 5HE
*e-mail* ylolfa@ylolfa.com
*website* www.ylolfa.com
*tel* 01970 832 304
*fax* 832 782

Teach
Your Dog
Cornish

"Hello"

# "Fatla genes"

pron:

## "Fat-la gen-ez"

'ge'
as in
'get'

"Come here"

**"Deus omma"**

*pron:*

**"D<u>uh</u>-z <u>omma</u>"**

'uh'
as in
'<u>ur</u>n'

rhymes
with
'comma'

"Don't!"

"Na wra henna!"

pron:

"Na _rah_ henna!"

'ah' as in 'f_a_ther'

"Do you want
a cuddle?"

"A vyn'ta
byrlans?"

pron:

"A vin-ta
beer-lanz?"

'a'
as in
'ago'

pronounce
this 'r'

'a'
as in
'ago'

"Catch!"

"Kach e!"

pron:
"Catch e!"

'e'
as in
'met'

"Fetch!"

"Kergh e!"

pron:

"Cair-h e!"

'ai' as in 'hair'

pronounce this 'r'

'e' as in 'met'

"Leave it!"

"Gas e!"

*pron:*

"G<u>ah</u>z <u>e</u>!"

'ah'
as in
'f<u>a</u>ther'

'e'
as in
'm<u>e</u>t'

"Sit!"

"Esedh!"

pron:
"Ez-eth!"

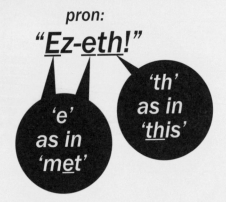

'e'
as in
'met'

'th'
as in
'this'

"No!"

"Na!"

pron:
"N<u>ah</u>!"

'ah'
as in
'f<u>a</u>ther'

"Stay!"

**"Gorta!"**

*pron:*

*"Gore-ta!"*

*pronounce this 'r'*

*'a' as in 'ago'*

"Bathtime"

## "Prys bath"

*pron:*

*"Preez ba̱t̲h̲"*

'a'
as in
'ma̱n'

'th'
as in
't̲h̲in'

"Bedtime"

**"Prys gweli"**

*pron:*
**"Preez gwell-ee"**

"Lunchtime"

"Prys li"

*pron:*

*"Preez lee"*

"Are you full?"

"Os ta leun?"

pron:
"Oss ta l<u>uh</u>n?"

'uh'
as in
'<u>u</u>rn'

"All gone"

"Gyllys yw e"

*pron:*

"*Gill-iz yoo e*"

'e'
as in
'met'

"Good morning"

"Myttin da"

*pron:*

*"Mitt-in d<u>ah</u>"*

'ah'
as in
'f<u>a</u>ther'

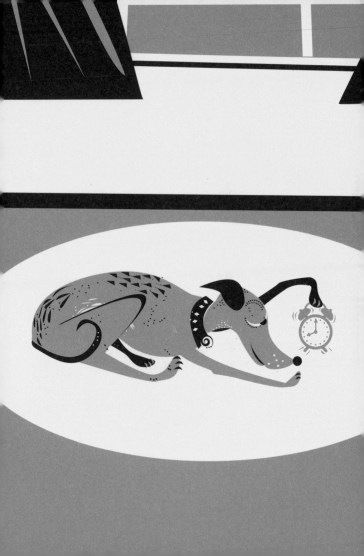

"Goodnight"

**"Nos da"**

*pron:*
**"Nohs d<u>ah</u>"**

'ah'
as in
'f<u>a</u>ther'

"Don't scratch"

"Na wra kravas"

pron:
"Na rah <u>crav</u>-<u>az</u>"

emphasise this syllable

'a' as in 'm<u>a</u>n'

"Let's go..."

"Deun ni..."

pron:

"Duhn nee..."

'uh'
as in
'urn'

"Go down"

"Ke yn-nans"

*pron:*

**"Keh in-nanz"**

'eh'
as in 'hair'
– but don't
pronounce
the 'r'

'a'
as in
'man'

"Up you go"

"Ke yn-bann"

pron:
"K<u>eh</u> in-ban"

'eh'
as in 'h<u>air</u>'
– but don't
pronounce
the 'r'

"Go straight ahead"

**"Ke yn-rag"**

*pron:*
**"Keh in-rag"**

'eh'
as in 'hair'
– but don't
pronounce
the 'r'

"Go left"

"Ke a-gledh"

*pron:*

"Keh a-gleh-th"

'a'
as in
'a<u>go</u>'

'eh'
as in 'h<u>ai</u>r'
– but don't
pronounce
the 'r'

'th'
as in
'<u>th</u>is'

"Go right"

"Ke a-dhyghow"

pron:

"Keh a-thee-who"

'eh'
as in 'hair'
– but don't
pronounce
the 'r'

'th'
as in
'this'

'a'
as in
'ago'

"Turn left"

# "Treyl a-gledh"

*pron:*

**"Tray-l a-gleh-th"**

'a' as in 'a<u>go</u>'

'eh' as in 'h<u>air</u>' – but don't pronounce the 'r'

'th' as in '<u>this</u>'

"Turn right"

**"Treyl a-dhyghow"**

*pron:*
**"Tray-l a-thee-who"**

'a' as in 'ago'

'th' as in 'this'

"Get down!"

**"Yn-nans!"**

pron:

**"In-nanz!"**

'a'
as in
'man'

"Do you
want to play?"

"A vyn'ta
gwari?"

*pron:*

"A vin-ta gwa-r-ee?"

'a'
as in
'ago'

'a'
as in
'man'

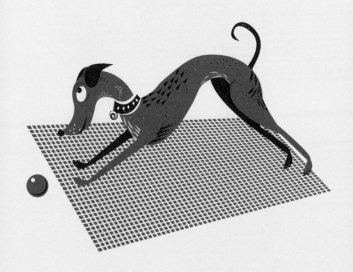

"Lie down!"

"Gorwedh!"

pron:

"Gor-weth!"

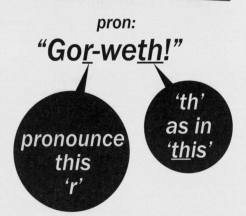

pronounce this 'r'

'th' as in 'this'

"Say 'please'!"

"Lavar 'mar pleg'!"

*pron:*

*"La-vahr 'ma-r pleh-g'!"*

*pronounce this 'r'*

*'eh' as in 'hair' – but don't pronounce the 'r'*

"Can I have the ball?"

## "A allav vy kavos an bel?"

pron:

## "A al-av ee kav-oz ann beh-l?"

'a' as in 'man'

'eh' as in 'hair' – but don't pronounce the 'r'

'a' as in 'man'

"Can I have a pasty?"

"A allav vy kavos pasti?"

pron:

"A al-av ee kav-oz pahs-tee?"

'a' as in 'man'

'ah' as in 'father'

"It's warm"

"Tomm yw hi"

pron:
"Tom yoo hee"

"It's cold"

**"Yeyn yw hi"**

*pron:*
**"Yay-n yoo hee"**

"It's hot"

"Pooth yw hi"

pron:

"Pow-th yoo hee"

'ow'
as in
'bowl'

'th'
as in
'thin'

"It's raining"

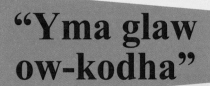

"Yma glaw
ow-kodha"

pron:

"Uh-<u>mah</u>
<u>glou</u>
owe-<u>co</u>-<u>tha</u>"

emphasise
this
syllable

'co'
as in
'<u>cot</u>'

'th'
as in
'<u>this</u>'

'lou'
as in
'<u>loud</u>'

"Are you happy?"

"Os ta lowen?"

pron:
"Oss ta low-en?"

"Who's snoring?"

## "Piw eus ow renki?"

pron:

*"Pyoo uh-z owe r__e__nk-ee?"*

'e'
as in
'm__e__t'

"Have you got
enough room?"

**"Eus lowr
a spas genes?"**

*pron:*
**"Uh-z low-r
<u>a</u> spa-ss g<u>e</u>n-ez?"**

'a'
as in
'a<u>go</u>'

'ge'
as in
'g<u>e</u>t'

"I won't be long"

"Ny vedhav vy pell"

pron:

"Nee v<u>e</u>th-<u>a</u>v ee p<u>e</u>ll"

'e' as in 'm<u>e</u>t'

'th' as in '<u>th</u>is'

'a' as in 'm<u>a</u>n'

'e' as in 'm<u>e</u>t'

"Be quiet!"

"Taw!"

pron:
"Tow!"

'ow'
as in
'cow'

"Who did that?"

"Piw a wrug henna?"

*pron:*

"Pyoo <u>a</u> reeg h<u>e</u>nna?"

'a' as in '<u>a</u>go'

'e' as in 'm<u>e</u>t'

"There's a queue for the loo"

**"Yma lost dhe'n bisva"**

pron:
"Uh-<u>mah</u> lost then bees-va"

emphasise this syllable

# 1

## "onan"

*pron:*

## "o-nen"

'o'
as in
'h**o**t'

# 2

## "dew"

*pron:*

## "de-w"

'e'
as in
'm**e**t'

'w'
as in
'co**w**'

3

"**trí**"

*pron:*
"**tree**"

4

"**peswar**"

*pron:*
"*pez-wah̲r*"

*pronounce
this 'r'*

9

"**naw**"

*pron:*
"*now*"

"Thank you"

## "Meur ras"

*pron:*

"M**uh**-r r**ah**-ss"

'uh'
as in
'**u**rn'

'ah'
as in
'f**a**ther'

pronounce
this 'r'

"Merry Christmas"

## "Nadelek Lowen"

*pron:*

**"Na-dell-ek Low-en"**

'a' as in 'man'

'e' as in 'met'

"Happy Birthday"

"Pennbloodh
Lowen"

pron:
"Pen-bl<u>ow</u>-<u>th</u>
Low-en"

'ow'
as in
'b<u>ow</u>l'

'th'
as in
'<u>th</u>is'

"I love you"

# "My a'th kar"

*pron:*

***"Mee ah-th car"***

'th' as in 'thin'

pronounce this 'r'

"Goodbye"

## "Dyw genes"

pron:

## "Dyoo gen-ez"

'ge'
as in
'get'

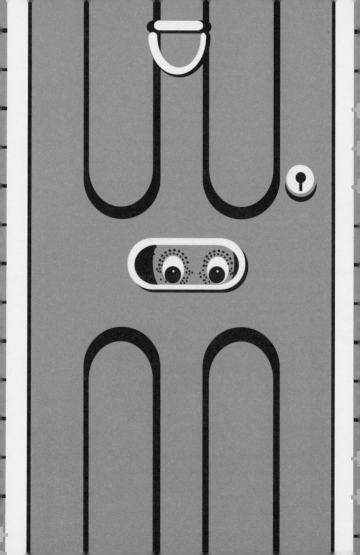

Other titles in this series include:

Teach Your Dog Welsh
Teach Your Cat Welsh
Teach Your Dog Irish
Teach Your Dog Māori
Teach Your Dog Japanese
(Rugby World Cup 2019 Travel Edition)